Trends in Southeast Asia

2016 no. 16

Trends in Southeast Asia

THE JOHOR SULTANATE:
RISE OR RE-EMERGENCE?

FRANCIS E. HUTCHINSON AND
VANDANA PRAKASH NAIR

 YUSOF ISHAK
INSTITUTE

Published by: ISEAS Publishing
                  30 Heng Mui Keng Terrace
                  Singapore 119614
                  publish@iseas.edu.sg http://bookshop.iseas.edu.sg

ISEAS Library Cataloguing-in-Publication Data

Hutchinson, Francis E.
   The Johor Sultanate : Rise or Re-emergence?
   (Trends in Southeast Asia, 0219-3213 ; TRS 16/16)
   1. Ibrahim Ismail, Sultan of Johor.
   2. Sultans—Malaysia—Johor.
   3. Johor—Politics and government.
   I. Title.
   II. Nair, Vandana Prakash.
   III. Series: Trends in Southeast Asia ; TRS 16/16.
DS501 I59T no. 16(2016)   November 2016

ISBN 978-981-47-6279-3 (soft cover)
ISBN 978-981-47-6280-9 (e-book, PDF)

Typeset by Superskill Graphics Pte Ltd
Printed in Singapore by Mainland Press Pte Ltd

FOREWORD

The economic, political, strategic and cultural dynamism in Southeast Asia has gained added relevance in recent years with the spectacular rise of giant economies in East and South Asia. This has drawn greater attention to the region and to the enhanced role it now plays in international relations and global economics.

The sustained effort made by Southeast Asian nations since 1967 towards a peaceful and gradual integration of their economies has had indubitable success, and perhaps as a consequence of this, most of these countries are undergoing deep political and social changes domestically and are constructing innovative solutions to meet new international challenges. Big Power tensions continue to be played out in the neighbourhood despite the tradition of neutrality exercised by the Association of Southeast Asian Nations (ASEAN).

The **Trends in Southeast Asia** series acts as a platform for serious analyses by selected authors who are experts in their fields. It is aimed at encouraging policy makers and scholars to contemplate the diversity and dynamism of this exciting region.

THE EDITORS

Series Chairman:
    Tan Chin Tiong

Series Editors:
    Ooi Kee Beng
    Lee Hock Guan

Editorial Committee:
    Terence Chong
    Francis E. Hutchinson
    Daljit Singh

Copy Editors:
    Veena Nair
    Kenneth Poon Jian Li

The Johor Sultanate: Rise or Re-emergence?

By Francis E. Hutchinson and Vandana Prakash Nair

EXECUTIVE SUMMARY

- Malaysia's sultans have in recent years taken on an increasingly discernible role in the country's political life. However, rather than something new, the rulers' resurgence should be viewed as part of a longer term negotiation over the precise boundaries of their role.
- The Sultan of Johor, Ibrahim Ismail, is arguably the most visible of the country's rulers at present. Since ascending to the throne in 2010, he has constructed a prominent media profile and been active in many areas of policy-making. He reinstated the Islamic week, suggested expanding the role of the Johor Military Force, and promoted a unique state identity. Planned initiatives by him include a Bank of Johor, a large-scale low-cost housing scheme, as well as a maglev train linking the eastern and western parts of the state's southern coast.
- Sultan Ibrahim Ismail has also weighed in on national-level issues, such as the quality of national education and bilateral relations with Singapore.
- While the more ceremonial aspects of his actions are inspired by the pivotal role traditionally played by Malay rulers, the more operational aspects hark back to the colonial era when Johor had a reputation for modern administration, well-developed infrastructure, and a high degree of autonomy.
- At its core, the Sultan raises questions about Malay leadership, and may revive a long-standing contest between the rulers and the political elite, sometimes referred to as a battle between "princes and politicians".

The Johor Sultanate: Rise or Re-emergence?

By Francis E. Hutchinson and Vandana Prakash Nair[1]

PLANES, TRAINS AND AUTOMOBILES

Malaysia is a monarchy — albeit one that is *sui generis*. Rather than following a single line of succession, the kingship rotates among a group of traditional rulers — or sultans — who head nine of the country's thirteen states. Although some of the sultanates pre-date the arrival of Islam in the region, they are now closely associated with the religion and have been a part of the Malayan peninsula's political context for 600 years.

During the pre-colonial and colonial eras, the rulers had a wide scope of prerogatives but many of these were relinquished during Malaysia's transition to independence. At present, the sultans are ceremonial rulers, and executive power rests with the prime minister at the national level, and chief ministers and menteris besar at the state level. That said, they are responsible for religion and Malay culture within their respective states, while their historic and symbolic importance as well as a number of constitutional provisions allow their influence to extend significantly further.

Over the past few years, these rulers have begun to assume a more visible role in the country's political life. In some states, they have chosen to withhold their consent for the appointment of menteris besar and, in Perak in 2009, the sultan played a decisive role in toppling the coalition

---

[1] Francis E. Hutchinson is Senior Fellow and Vandana Prakash Nair is Research Officer at the ISEAS – Yusof Ishak Institute, Singapore.

in power.[2] Collectively, the sultans have also weighed in on national-level issues such as the quality of governance and rule of law.[3]

Of the traditional rulers, the Sultan of Johor, Ibrahim Ismail, has been arguably the most notable. Part of his public persona revolves around his extensive collection of vehicles. He recently purchased a blue and gold 737 Boeing, which will be used to "promote Johor" and allow him to travel the world like his ancestors "who once travelled around in ships".[4] He has also given another plane to the Johor soccer team, which is owned by his eldest son, the Crown Prince.[5]

The Sultan was also the first of the rulers to obtain a locomotive driving licence, and he piloted the last Malayan Railway train out of Tanjong Pagar Station in Singapore in 2011.[6] A long-time automobile aficionado, he has a collection of some 300 units.[7] In 2015, he became the owner of the world's most expensive Mack truck, outfitted with a six-camera CCTV system, two flat-screen televisions, a kitchen, as well as a bed and seats with 72,000 stitches of gold thread.[8]

---

[2] Shad Saleem Faruqi, "The 2009 Constitutional Turmoil in Perak: A Look Back", in *Perak: A State of Crisis*, edited by Audrey Quay (Petaling Jaya: Loyar Burok Publications, 2010), p. 145.

[3] "Malay Rulers Want 1MDB Issue Settled Soonest, Demand Report", *BorneoPost Online*, 7 October 2015 <http://www.theborneopost.com/2015/10/07/malay-rulers-want-1mdb-issue-settled-soonest-demand-report/> (accessed 24 October 2016).

[4] "Sultan Receives his New Aircraft", *Star Online,* 1 March 2016 <http://www.thestar.com.my/news/nation/2016/03/01/sultan-receives-his-new-aircraft-medical-grads-issue-to-drag-on-the-plane-touched-down-at-senai-afte/> (accessed 24 October 2016).

[5] "JDT Football Team Gets Private Jet from Johor Sultan", *Rakyat Post,* 2 August 2016.

[6] "Sultan Ibrahim is the first Ruler to get a Train Driver's License", *Star Online,* 29 June 2010.

[7] "Sultan of Johor Shows Kris His Motorcycle, Car Collection", YouTube video, 11:33, posted by ABS-CBN News, 17 June 2013 <https://www.youtube.com/watch?v=ssBJuBIL5Pc> (accessed 24 October 2016).

[8] "Sultan of Johor buys 'Palace Truck'", *Straits Times*, 17 October 2016.

Sultan Ibrahim Ismail has also weighed in on policy matters and issues affecting public life, from religion and culture to inter-ethnic relations, and from land management to education. He and the Crown Prince have frequently commented on the historical and cultural specificity of the state, encapsulated in the term *Bangsa Johor*, which implies an identity based on territory and local culture — as opposed to ethnicity. The Crown Prince has provocatively stated that Johor could imagine seceding from the Malaysian Federation, under certain conditions.[9]

Some of these issues fall within the strict constitutional role prescribed for traditional rulers, largely relating to Malay religion and custom. Others involve operational issues or national-level policies, and — to some — the Sultan's comments extend beyond the role currently specified for the rulers in the Constitution. According to experts in history and constitutional law, the Constitution does not allow for the withdrawal of any state from the Federation.[10]

However, even if education, health and bilateral relations are outside the remit of traditional rulers, these were matters of routine interest for them before independence. At a deeper level, this diversity in opinions means that while the traditional rulers are a central part of the political milieu, the precise contours of their role are not immutable.

This paper examines the Sultan of Johor's recent public statements, in light of the current political context and with reference to the state's history. It argues that his actions and comments are guided by a very specific understanding of the role of a Malay ruler which is rooted in history. First, in ceremonial aspects, clear reference is made to the role of sultans in the pre-colonial and colonial eras, particularly their symbolic importance and how they participated in public life. Second, in areas pertaining to policy, inspiration is drawn from the sultanate of Johor during the colonial era, which had a reputation for modern and

---

[9] "Crown prince: Johor has Right to Withdraw from M'sia", *New Paper*, 17 October 2015.

[10] Wan Syamsul Amly, "Johor Secession No Longer Possible after Merdeka", *Astro Awani*, 18 June 2015; "Malaysia Charter doesn't Provide for Secession", *Straits Times*, 20 October 2015.

efficient administration, multi-ethnic subjects, and a significant degree of autonomy. Taken together, these references imply a more expansive role for the Sultan of Johor in particular, and traditional rulers more generally, than had been the case in the recent past. This development could rekindle a long-running competition in Malaysia between the royalty and Malay political elites, or what some have termed the rivalry between "princes and politicians".[11]

Following this introduction, the role and prerogatives of the sultans today are examined. From there, how the Sultan of Johor has participated in political life will be analysed, in particular: how his authority is displayed in the public sphere; what domains of state-level policy he has sought to influence; and how he has intervened in national-level issues. The last section will look into the future.

MALAYSIA AND ITS SULTANS

As a constitutional monarchy, Malaysia is headed by a king, with an elected parliament and prime minister. The sultans[12] are the constitutional heads of their respective states, and state governments — led by elected chief ministers and state legislative assemblies — have responsibilities that include religion and Malay custom, land management, natural resources, and local government.[13]

---

[11] This term was coined by A.J. Stockwell in "Princes and Politicians: The Constitutional Crisis in Malaysia, 1983–84", in *Constitutional Head and Political Crises*, edited by D.A. Low (London: Palgrave Macmillan, 1988), pp. 182–97.

[12] Malaysia has nine Malay rulers, from the states of Perlis, Kedah, Kelantan, Terengganu, Perak, Negri Sembilan, Selangor, Pahang, and Johor. While the majority are referred to as "Sultans", the rulers of Perlis and Negri Sembilan are referred to as "Raja" and "Yang di-Pertuan", respectively. For simplicity, the terms "sultans" and "traditional" or "Malay rulers" will be used.

[13] J.C. Fong, *Constitutional Federalism in Malaysia* (Kuala Lumpur: Sweet and Maxwell Asia, 2008), chapters 3 and 4. Sabah and Sarawak, due to their later incorporation into the Federation, have a more extensive list of responsibilities.

The Constitution lays out the responsibilities and prerogatives of the Malay Rulers. While these have since been subject to debate, the king and sultans had the following prerogatives at the time of independence:[14]

- Legislation passed in parliament and state legislative assemblies required their assent to be passed.
- They could block requests to dissolve parliament or state legislative assemblies.
- They had the right to name the prime minister or menteri besar that, in their judgement, commanded the confidence of the majority party in parliament or state legislative assembly.
- They (but not their families) had legal immunity in their public and personal capacities.

The king also had the following national-level responsibilities:

- the authority to declare a state of emergency, upon advice from the prime minister; and
- the authority to appoint and remove members of organisations such as the Public Services Commission, the Judicial and Legal Services Commission, Election Commission, and Police Force Commission, as well as judges of the superior courts.

Furthermore, sultans had the following prerogatives within the confines of their respective states:

---

[14] This section draws on the following: Vincent Lowe, "Symbolic Communication in Malaysian Politics — the case of the Sultanate", *Southeast Asian Journal of Social Science* 10, no. 2 (1982): 71–89; Raja Azlan Shah, "The Role of Constitutional Rulers in Malaysia", in *The Constitution in Malaysia: Further Perspectives and Developments*, edited by Francis A. Trindade and Hoong Phun Lee (Singapore: Oxford University Press, 1986), pp. 76–91; Andrew Harding, *Law, Government, and the Constitution in Malaysia* (The Hague: Kluwer Law International, 1996); Andrew Harding, *The Constitution of Malaysia: A Contextual Analysis* (Oxford: Hart Publishing, 2012); and Shad Saleem Faruqi, *Document of Destiny: The Constitution of the Federation of Malaysia* (Petaling Jaya: Star Publications, 2008).

- the right to name members of the State Executive Council upon the advice of the menteri besar;
- exclusive control over Islam and Malay custom, and state-level religious bureaucracies; and
- the authority to award honours and grant pardons.

Beyond their individual privileges, the sultans have also had a number of collective responsibilities. The Conference of Rulers is a policy body that brings together the Rulers, their menteris besar, the governors and chief ministers of Penang, Malacca, Sabah, and Sarawak,[15] and the king and prime minister. While it has no means of compulsion, the Conference can do the following:

- discuss and deliberate on matters of national importance; and
- provide advice on any public service appointment, particularly relating to the judiciary, as well as the Auditor-General, and key organizations such as the Election Commission and Public Services Commission.

In addition, on matters pertaining to the Malay Rulers, only the king and sultans are allowed to attend the Council, and have the following prerogatives:

- decide who will be king and, if necessary, remove him by majority vote;
- approve any law relating to the privileges and position of the Malay rulers; and
- intervene in determining state boundaries.

---

[15] Penang, Malacca, Sabah and Sarawak do not have menteris besar and sultans. The elected political leaders are referred to as chief ministers, and ceremonial leadership is vested in governors, who are appointed for four-year terms by the king on advice from the respective chief minister. Raja Azlan Shah, *The Role of Constitutional Rulers in Malaysia*, p. 77.

Beyond the explicit constitutional stipulations, the sultanates also enjoy enormous social and political capital. They are seen as symbols of Malay culture in general and Malay rights in particular.

Furthermore, in recognition of the Malay Rulers' long history, the Constitution states that the "sovereignty, prerogatives, powers and jurisdiction of the Rulers … as hitherto had and enjoyed shall remain unaffected".[16] While open to interpretation, this text implies that the sultanates are pre-existing institutions whose reach goes beyond what is outlined in the Constitution.[17]

Beyond these prerogatives, the position of the Malay Rulers in public life is sacrosanct, and protected by a range of coercive measures. The Sedition Act prohibits any action or statement that can "bring into hatred or contempt or to excite disaffection against any Ruler or against any government".[18]

The extent of the Rulers' responsibilities and prerogatives were central to negotiations held prior to independence. The nationalist elite — led by the United Malays National Organisation (UMNO) — differed with the sultans on the role that the latter were to have. While recognizing the symbolic importance of the sultans, UMNO's leaders, with strong support from the Malay ground, held most of the aces in the talks with the Rulers and the British.[19]

---

[16] Article 181 of the Malaysian Constitution, cited in Harding, *Law, Government, and the Constitution in Malaysia*, p. 65.

[17] Anthony Milner, *The Evolution of the Malaysian Monarchy, and the Bonding of the Nation* (Bangi: Penerbit Universiti Kebangsaan Malaysia, 2011), p. 18.

[18] Lowe, *Symbolic Communication in Malaysian Politics*, p. 79; H.F. Rawlings, "The Malaysian Constitutional Crisis of 1983", *International and Comparative Law Quarterly* 35 (1986): 248.

[19] Chandra Muzaffar, *Protector? An Analysis of the Concept and Practice of Loyalty in Leader-led Relationships within Malay Society* (Penang: Aliran, 1979); Donna Amoroso, *Traditionalism and the Ascendancy of the Malay Ruling Class in Colonial Malaya* (Singapore: NUS Press, 2014).

What the nationalist elite wanted was a strong central government to drive economic development, as well as an independent judiciary, and were reluctant to have strong state governments after independence. Disagreements arose over financial provisions for the states and their sultans, as well as the remit of the Conference of Rulers. In the end, UMNO was compelled to yield more financial autonomy to the states and a wider political role for the Conference than initially desired.[20]

The role of the sultans increased further in the wake of the 1969 riots. As part of a broader move towards bolstering the position of the Malays, in 1971 the Constitution was amended to require the assent of the Conference of Rulers for any change to the provisions relating to sensitive issues such as the national language, religion, as well as the position of the Malays and indigenous Sabahans and Sarawakians.[21]

However, the prerogatives and responsibilities of the sultans were subsequently circumscribed, due to two structural dynamics. First, relations between Malaysia's political leadership — particularly UMNO — and the Rulers came under tension in the 1970s. In Johor, Perak, and Pahang, disagreements arose over the choice of menteris besar in their respective states. In the case of Pahang, the sultan used his ability to block state-level legislation for two years in protest. In all three cases, the unwanted ministers eventually resigned. For some, the monarch's influence in these cases clearly went beyond the intention of the Constitution.[22]

Second, the country's elected leadership underwent a generational change. The first prime minister, Tunku Abdul Rahman, was part of the Kedah royalty, while the second and third came from aristocratic circles in Pahang and Johor. In contrast, the fourth prime minister, Mahathir

---

[20] Joseph Fernando, *The Making of the Malayan Constitution* (Kuala Lumpur: Malayan Branch of the Royal Asiatic Society, 2002), pp. 169–74.

[21] Milner, *The Evolution of the Malaysian Monarchy, and the Bonding of the Nation*, p. 17.

[22] Rawlings, "The Malaysian Constitutional Crisis of 1983", p. 245.

Mohamed, was a commoner firmly wedded to the notion that the sultans should retain only a ceremonial role, arguing that "in practice the King and the Rulers held significant power and authority which could negate the democratic principle of government by the people".[23]

Given the procedures governing the rotation of the kingship, the Sultan of either Johor or Perak was slated to ascend to the throne in 1984. Seeking to circumscribe their room for manoeuvre and — perhaps as some have argued, seeking to remove a check on his authority — Mahathir attempted to amend the Constitution to reduce the monarchy's prerogatives in 1983. This entailed eliminating the constitutional checks the king and sultans had on vetoing legislation and transferring the authority to declare emergency rule from the king to the prime minister.[24]

Despite being passed in parliament, the bill also needed to be signed by the King. Although he had initially agreed, the King subsequently changed his mind. Following a prolonged stalemate, the provisions were watered down, before being passed by parliament and accepted by the Conference of Rulers. While the King was now only allowed to delay — but not block — legislation for a maximum of sixty days, he retained the ability to declare a state of emergency. In addition, sultans retained their veto of legislation at the state level, although they pledged not to use this prerogative.[25]

While that particular impasse may have been resolved, the Rulers still sought to influence their menteris besar and acted in ways that were thought by some to constitute interference.[26] In addition, the wider role of the sultans and their families led to public debate about a number

---

[23] Mahathir Mohamad, *A Doctor in the House: The Memoirs of Tun Dr Mahathir Mohamad* (Petaling Jaya: MPH Publishing 2011), p. 452.

[24] Barry Wain, *Malaysian Maverick: Mahathir Mohamad in Turbulent Times* (Basingstoke: Palgrave Macmillan 2009), p. 204.

[25] Rawlings, "The Malaysian Constitutional Crisis of 1983", pp. 251–53; Harding, *Law, Government, and the Constitution in Malaysia*, p. 75.

[26] Harding, *Law, Government, and the Constitution in Malaysia*, p. 76.

of issues such as: the *de facto* legal immunity enjoyed by the royalty at large; the extensive business interests of some sultans; and examples of profligacy and the implied cost to public coffers.[27] Furthermore, in 1992, Sultan Iskandar of Johor was alleged to have physically assaulted a member of the public.[28]

Following this, Mahathir acted to remove the Rulers' legal immunity as well as their ability to block legislation. Following intensive negotiations, including a variety of enticements and threats to the sultans, a constitutional amendment was passed in 1993. The Rulers were now no longer able to veto legislation at the state level; the authority to declare a state of emergency was bestowed upon the prime minister; and sultans no longer enjoyed legal immunity in their private capacities, although such trials were to take place in a special court. In addition, constraints on parliamentary discussions regarding the role of the Rulers were relaxed.[29]

For the remainder of Mahathir's tenure, there were no disagreements regarding the extent of royal prerogatives.[30] However, shortly after he stepped down in late 2003, the Rulers began again to play a more public role. In 2006, the Sultan of Selangor asked a state assemblyman to resign following the revelation of his involvement in a number of financial irregularities. The following year, the Conference of Rulers rejected Prime Minister Abdullah Badawi's nominated candidate for a high-ranking judicial position.[31]

---

[27] Muzaffar, *Protector? An Analysis of the Concept and Practice of Loyalty in Leader-led Relationships within Malay Society*, p. 74; Harding, *The Constitution of Malaysia: A Contextual Analysis*, pp. 118–19; Mahathir, *A Doctor in the House*, p. 453.

[28] Wain, *Malaysian Maverick: Mahathir Mohamad in Turbulent Times*, p. 209.

[29] Wain, ibid., pp. 209–10; Harding, *The Constitution of Malaysia: A Contextual Analysis*, pp. 120–21. A further amendment passed in 1994 reduced the amount of time the king could delay legislation from 60 to 30 days.

[30] Kobkua Suwannathat-Pian, *Palace, Political Party, and Power: A Story of the Socio-Political Development of Malay Kingship* (Singapore: NUS Press: 2011), p. 410.

[31] Ahmad Fauzi Abdul Hamid and Muhamad Rakiyuddin Ismail, "The Monarchy and Party Politics in Malaysia in the Era of Abdullah Ahmad Badawi (2003–09): The Resurgence of the Role of Protector", *Asian Survey* 52, no. 5 (2012): 931–32.

In 2008, the ruling coalition, Barisan Nasional, unprecedentedly lost five state governments. In addition to introducing more competition for office at the state level, this turn of events provided the sultans with an opportunity to exercise their discretionary powers. In Perlis and Terengganu, two states won by Barisan Nasional, the sultans passed over the nominated candidates in favour of other state assemblypersons.[32] The following year, with three state legislators crossing the floor, the Sultan of Perak opted to name a menteri besar from the opposing coalition, rather than calling for fresh elections.[33] And in 2014, the Sultan of Selangor blocked the incumbent coalition's initial nomination for menteri besar and subsequently called for a selection of names to be put forward for his consideration.[34]

Public debates ensued on the role of the Rulers. On one hand, there were calls for the sultans to refrain from engaging in politics, and to remain as ceremonial leaders.[35] On the other, the Sultan of Perak, Nazrin Shah, argued that beyond the aspects of unifying the nation and representing Malay culture and religion, the country's monarchy should contribute to public life through promoting good governance and the rule of law, as well as checking extremism.[36]

THE SULTANATE OF JOHOR

Johor is the country's southern-most state, bordering on Singapore. Its flat fertile land has been particularly suited to agriculture, and the state has

---

[32] Ahmad Fauzi Abdul Hamid and Muhamad Takyudin Ismail, ibid., p. 934.

[33] "Perak in Crisis: Sultan tells Nizar, Exco to Resign", *New Straits Times*, 2 May 2009.

[34] Bernard Cheah and Aiezat Fadzell, "Azmin is Sultan's Choice for Selangor MB", *Sun Daily*, 22 September 2014.

[35] Abdul Aziz Bari, *The Monarchy and the Constitution in Malaysia* (Kuala Lumpur: IDEAS, 2013), pp. 334–35; Muaz Omar, "In Defence of Monarchy … Minus the Politics", *The Malaysian Insider*, 11 February 2009.

[36] Raja Nazrin Shah, *The Monarchy in Contemporary Malaysia* (Singapore: Institute of Southeast Asian Studies, 2004).

long been a key source of capital and foreign exchange for Malaysia. In population terms, Johor is the second largest in the country and also has the second largest number of parliamentary constituencies. It occupies a central place in Malay politics, as UMNO was founded in the state and it has contributed a disproportionate number of the first generation of independence leaders.[37] Even today, the state has the largest number of UMNO party members — estimated at some 400,000 people.[38]

In addition, the state has always had dynamic sultans who vowed to make Johor "the greatest Malay power, to keep her free, and to make her rich".[39] From the 1840s onwards, its rulers proved particularly adept at laying claim to increasing amounts of land, cultivating relations with other sultans and polities, and lobbying London for more recognition and prerogatives.[40]

Of particular note are two sultans. The first, Abu Bakar, reigned from 1862 to 1895 and is credited with developing many of Johor's unique institutions. Unlike the Federated Malay States (FMS) of Negri Sembilan, Pahang, Selangor and Perak, which came under direct British influence in the 1870s and 1880s, Johor held out against external control until the early twentieth century. Given the sultanate's proximity to Singapore and the FMS, Abu Bakar observed and adapted many British conventions to suit his particular circumstances. By the 1890s, Johor had developed an efficient and rules-based bureaucracy that provided an extensive array of social services, managed an army, navy, and postal system, and

---

[37] Francis E. Hutchinson, "Malaysia's Independence Leaders and the Legacies of State Formation under British Rule", *Journal of the Royal Asiatic Society* 3, no. 25 (2015): 123–51.

[38] Interview with Nur Jazlan, UMNO MP for Pulai, Johor Bahru, Malaysia, 18 May 2010.

[39] Eunice Thio, "British Policy towards Johore", *JMBRAS* 40, no. 1 (1967): 11.

[40] For a comprehensive account of the development of the Sultanate of Johor in the nineteenth century, please consult Carl A. Trocki, *Prince of Pirates: Temenggongs and the Development of Johor and Singapore, 1784–1885* (Singapore: NUS Press, 2007).

had a quasi-diplomatic body in London to lobby parliament.[41] In 1895, the sultanate was the first to draft its own constitution, which blended elements of Malay custom with British law and governance structures.[42]

The second sultan, Ibrahim, ruled from 1895 until 1959, and is remembered for his negotiations with both the British and the nationalist elite to preserve a maximum degree of autonomy for Johor. Although Johor was compelled to accept a British adviser in 1910 and assign him substantial responsibilities in 1914, the sultanate was able to secure important concessions such as: the right to dismiss undesired British officers; retaining preference in government employment for Johor Malays; and preserving Malay, along with English, as the language of government.[43] As a result, the Sultan was able to retain control over strategic areas of government, with many key positions and departments remaining in the hands of his subjects. In addition, he prioritized commodity production, which allowed the state to generate high revenue streams, much of which were subsequently invested in infrastructure and social services. Indeed, due to substantial fiscal prudence, the sultanate ran a budget surplus from 1918 until World War II.[44]

On their return after the Japanese Occupation, the British sought to replace the various Malay States and Straits Settlements with the Malayan Union in 1946. This would have vested most responsibilities

---

[41] Hutchinson, "Malaysia's Independence Leaders and the Legacies of State Formation", pp. 135–57; Mohd Sarim Haji Mustajab, "The Impact of Colonial Rule in Johor: A Case of Social and Political Adjustment" (PhD Dissertation, University of Kent, 1985), pp. 96–101; *The Singapore and Straits Directory 1893* (Singapore: The Singapore and Straits Printing Office, 1893).

[42] James de Vere Allen, Anthony John Stockwell, and Leigh R. Wright, *A Collection of Treaties and Other Documents Affecting the States of Malaysia 1761–1963*, Vol. 1 (London: Oceana Publications, 1981), p. 76.

[43] de Vere Allen, Stockwell, and Wright, *A Collection of Treaties*, pp. 108–109.

[44] Ichiro Sugimoto, "An Analysis of the State of Johore's Finances 1910–1940", *JMBRAS* 80, no. 2 (2007): 70; "Appendix E: Revenue and Expenditure by Departments", in *Annual Report for Johor 1932* (Singapore: Government Printing Office, 1933).

and services in a strong central government, and transferred sovereignty from the Rulers to the British crown. This generated such widespread resistance in the Malay community that the Union had to be replaced by the Malaysian Federation in 1948.[45]

As part of this process, the British signed nine state agreements with each of the sultans to create the new Federation. Sultan Ibrahim thus signed the Johore Agreement of 1948, and a supplementary piece of legislation updated the state's Constitution to bring it in line with the Federal Constitution. The general effect this had was to reduce the Sultan's remit to Islam and Malay custom while expanding the role of the state government beyond the advisory and administrative role envisioned in Johor's 1895 Constitution.[46] This, however, did not stop Sultan Ibrahim from taking direct interest in affairs of government and promoting the state's interest through lobbying the British for increased infrastructure expenditure, more financial autonomy, and a return of Johorean civil servants that had joined the Malayan Civil Service.[47]

Yet, this same desire for autonomy led Sultan Ibrahim to oppose Johor's independence from Britain. During the celebrations for the sixtieth year of his reign in 1955 — and at the height of negotiations between Malaya's nationalist elite and the British over the timetable for their withdrawal — he questioned the wisdom of seeking independence during the Emergency. In response, UMNO leaders boycotted the celebrations and passed a motion of censure in the Johor legislative assembly.[48] The Sultan also resisted the withdrawal of the British adviser from Johor, arguing that his input was necessary for affairs to "run

---

[45] Anthony John Stockwell, *British Policy and Malay Politics during the Malayan Union Experiment, 1942–1948* (Kuala Lumpur: MBRAS, 1979).

[46] The Johore Agreement 1948 and Supplement to the Constitution 1367.

[47] Memorandum from Sultan Ibrahim to Donald MacGillivray, British High Commissioner to Malaya, 13 June 1954.

[48] "The Sultan Warns: 'If the British Leave …'", *Sunday Express*, 15 September 1955; "Sultan of Johore Censured", *Daily Telegraph*, 14 December 1955.

smoothly".[49] And in late 1955, one of the Sultan's cousins established a movement to advocate for the state's secession from Malaya and a return to its status as a British protectorate. Ignored by the nationalist leaders as well as the other traditional rulers, the movement was eclipsed when the Crown Prince of Johor signed the Federal Constitution in July 1957.[50]

Thus, it is with this legacy of strong leadership, hands-on policy-making, and a desire for autonomy that Sultan Ibrahim Ismail ascended to the Johor throne in 2010.

The subsequent sections look at the effects of this legacy in the following domains: the public portrayal of sultanate; the state-level issues and policies the Sultan has dealt with; and, how he has sought to intervene in national-level issues.

The Public Portrayal of the Sultanate

Taking place more than five years after he ascended to the throne, the Sultan's coronation in March 2015 was an elaborate affair. It consisted of a month-long celebration with visits to each of the state's ten districts. There were nine key events, which included open-air concerts, fireworks displays, a boat parade, a carnival and assorted sporting competitions.

The coronation itself took place in the throne room of the main palace in Johor, the Istana Besar. The Mufti of Johor, the head of the state's religious establishment, placed a 1.6 kilogramme crown topped by an Islamic crescent on the Sultan's head. Crafted by a London-based jeweller, the silver and gold crown was adorned with sapphires, emeralds, rubies, and diamonds. The Sultan's wife was crowned with a diamond-studded tiara of white gold. Both wore shoulder-length capes of blue silk, with inscriptions in gold thread.[51]

---

[49] Letter from Sultan Ibrahim to the British High Commissioner to Malaya, Donald MacGillivray, 1 December 1955.

[50] Nordin Sopiee, *From Malayan Union to Singapore Separation: Political Unification in the Malaysia Region, 1945–65* (Kuala Lumpur: Penerbit Universiti Malaya, 1975), pp. 80–85.

[51] Idayu Suparto, "10 Things to Know about the Celebrations to Mark the Johor Sultan's Coronation", *Straits Times*, 20 March 2015; "Johor Ruler's Coronation, A Royal Tradition with a Difference", *Sun Daily*, 2 March 2015.

Many aspects of this ritual are embedded in the history of the Malay rulers, particularly in the pre-colonial era. According to court chronicles and legal digests, sultans were the linchpin of society. They were imbued with immense ceremonial and religious power, and referred to with titles such as "God's shadow on earth".[52] When they assumed the throne, they were imbued with the *daulat* — majesty and sovereignty — that is the unique preserve of the royalty.[53]

As head of religion and custom, the sultans represented, preserved and enforced laws and traditions. Indeed, his subjects defined themselves by their societal position vis-à-vis the ruler, and it was also the ruler's obligation to name and treat his subjects according to the position that they occupied within this hierarchy. The sultan's role was so pivotal in society that "kerajaan", the term used for the sultanates at that time, literally signified "the condition" of having a raja or sultan.[54]

Wealth was central to the exercise of power, as it was through this medium that sultans were able to attract and retain followers. A person's rank and material wealth needed to be aligned, and the sultan, as foremost representative of his people, had to be "exceptional … in his manner of dress and accommodation". Sumptuary laws — customs governing what people wore — were extensive, with specific colours, textiles, and luxury items associated with, and reserved for, the royalty.[55]

This also extended to means of travel. Court annals noted when the rulers went travelling, with great importance being attached to the image they portrayed and how they were received in the host destination. For example, in 1885 when the Sultan of Terengganu travelled to Pahang for his wedding, he was accompanied by 400 people in a steamship, with

---

[52] Anthony Milner, "Islam and Malay Kingship", *Journal of the Royal Asiatic Society of Great Britain and Ireland* 1 (1981): 52.

[53] J.M. Gullick, *Indigenous Political Systems of Western Malaya* (Oxford: Berg, 2004), p. 45; Suwannathat-Pian, *Palace, Political Party, and Power*, p. 12.

[54] Anthony Milner, *Kerajaan: Malay Political Culture on the Eve of Colonial Rule* (Tucson: The University of Arizona Press, 1982), pp. 94–104.

[55] Anthony Milner, *The Malays* (Oxford: Wiley-Blackwell, 2011), pp. 60, 64–65.

1,000 more following in sail boats. Sultan Abu Bakar had an iron steamer and then a yacht for his travel, and also kept a large carriage. It is also recorded that in the sixteenth century, a "King" of Johor travelled at the head of a procession "leading all the city's people" atop an elephant.[56]

Beyond the Sultan's collection of vehicles mentioned above, the annual Kembara Mahkota Johor can be seen as a modern re-enactment of this tradition. Begun in 2001, when he was still Crown Prince, this tradition sees Sultan Ibrahim Ismail visiting Johor's ten districts at the head of a convoy of various vehicles, from motorbikes to four-wheel drives, and from trains to boats — the latter to access islands off the state's coast.[57]

Thus, the public portrayal of the Sultan of Johor is embedded in long-standing customs regarding the role that traditional rulers should play. While many of these practices date back centuries, they still resonate with substantial segments of Johorean society. In 2012, following his successful purchase of a car registration plate for RM520,000, the Sultan was criticized by a member of the Opposition for his supposed profligacy. In response to this, a crowd of an estimated 15,000 to 30,000 people marched to the Sultan's palace in a public display of support.[58]

---

[56] J.M. Gullick, *Rulers and Residents: Influence and Power in the Malay States* (Singapore: Oxford University Press, 1992), pp. 231–32; Abdul bin Abdul Kadir, *The Hikayat Abdullah* (Kuala Lumpur: Oxford University Press, 1970), p. 302. Peter Borschberg, ed., *Jacques de Coutre's Singapore and Johor 1594–1625* (Singapore: NUS Press), p. 51. We are grateful to Barbara Watson Andaya for her input on this point.

[57] Jasmine Shadique, "Joyous Meeting of the Sultan and his Subjects", *New Straits Times,* 25 March 2015; "Tiga Buah Trak Mewah Berlepas, Sultan Johor Mula Kembara Negeri" [Three trucks depart, the Sultan of Johor explores the state], *Malay Mail Online,* 14 May 2016; Mohd Farhaan Shah, "Ruler with a Personal Touch", *Star Online,* 4 June 2016.

[58] Mohd Farhaan Shah, "Johoreans March to Istana and Pledge Loyalty to Sultan over WWW1 Issue", *Star Online,* 11 June 2012. Sim Bak Heng and Jasmine Shadique, "Mind your own Business, Johor Ruler tells Critic", *New Straits Times,* 15 June 2012; "People remain loyal to Johor Sultan", YouTube video, 5:52, posted by Christine Leong, 11 June 2012 <https://www.youtube.com/watch?v=A1IWOPcNxJI> (accessed 24 October 2016).

State-level Policy Matters

Beyond the ceremonial element of his reign, Sultan Ibrahim Ismail has expressed opinions on a wide range of state-level issues and, on a number of occasions, assumed an operational role. In certain cases, these measures clearly fall within the remit of traditional rulers, but, in others, they imply a more hands-on role than had been the case in the recent past.

Religion and Malay Custom

In late 2013, the Sultan reinstated the Islamic week for government with effect from 1 January 2014, with the rationale that it would allow Muslims more time for their Friday prayers. This measure came as a surprise, as the state had long been known for its outward orientation and investment-friendly policy frameworks. In particular, private sector operations worried about the economic impact that this could have.[59]

That said, during the colonial period, Johor — along with the four northern Malay states — had observed the Islamic week. Indeed, it maintained this tradition until 1993, when the Johor state government made the decision to change the rest day from Friday to Sunday.[60] This measure was taken by the serving menteri besar as part of the wider push to curtail the sultans' prerogatives. In 1996, the current Sultan's father, Iskandar, urged the government to change the weekend back to Friday and Saturday, but with no success.[61]

While the reinstatement of the Islamic week can be seen as increasing the religious tenor of public life, Sultan Ibrahim has also made numerous appeals for moderation. He has called for Johor's inhabitants to avoid "deviant" teachings, and learn from religious teachers who possess

---

[59] Jason Ng, "Move to Alter Weekend Days Sparks Confusion in Malaysian State", *Wall Street Journal*, 2 December 2013.

[60] "Johor Sultan Has Power to Change Rest Day", *Malaysia Today*, 28 November 2013.

[61] "Johor Ruler Wants Weekend Changed Back to Friday", *Straits Times*, 10 February 1996.

proper credentials. In particular, Muslim preachers from outside Johor must be recognized by the Johor Islamic Religious Council (MAIJ).[62]

The Sultan has also made his influence felt on matters of Malay culture. He recently cautioned Malays against growing Arabization, encouraging them to retain their own culture instead of imitating outside influences, stating "If there are some of you who wish to be an Arab and practise Arab culture … that is up to you. I also welcome you to live in Saudi Arabia."[63]

In addition, he has sought to nuance the position of Malays in the country, relating it back to the Malay Rulers. Sultan Ibrahim Ismail stated that the term "Malay sovereignty" was more appropriate than "Malay supremacy" because it reflected the sovereignty of the Malay states with the Rulers at their apex. And while the concept of Malay sovereignty encompassed the position of the Malay Rulers, Islam as the Federation's official religion, Malay as the national language and Malay rights, it did not regard the other races as outsiders.[64]

As head of religion and Malay custom within the state, these declarations by the Sultan are fully within his purview, and are specified in the Johor Constitution.[65] They are also part of Johor royalty's long-established tradition of firm control over religious affairs. Sultan Abu Bakar, for example, invited renowned scholars to the state, established a religious hierarchy, and also accumulated texts of Islamic jurisprudence. Furthermore, during the colonial period, the British scrupulously avoided interference in religious matters. While many government departments

---

[62] "Sultan Johor: Learn Islam from those with Credentials", *New Straits Times*, 31 March 2016.

[63] "Stop Aping Arabs, Johor Sultan Tells Malays", *Malay Mail Online*, 24 March 2016.

[64] "Johor Sultan Calls for Rephrasing of 'Malay Supremacy' as 'Malay Sovereignty'", *Utusan Online*, 9 December 2010.

[65] Supplement to the Constitution of the State of Johore, no.43 A, XXB, 5 September 1957.

came to have British heads, this was never the case where religious matters were concerned.[66]

Bangsa Johor

The declarations on religion and Malay custom have also been accompanied by references to a unique state-level identity, expressed by the concept "Bangsa Johor". According to Sultan Ibrahim Ismail, the term was developed by Sultan Ibrahim in 1920, and expressed a shared commitment to the state's progress which transcends cultures and religion.[67]

These statements have been accompanied by a number of measures reaching out to Johor's various communities. In January 2016, the Sultan joined Hindu devotees during the Thaipusam celebration in Johor; and in February that year, he became the first Johor ruler to launch and attend the annual Chingay festival. In September 2016, he hosted a tea party in the Chinese Hall[68] in Johor's main palace to acknowledge the historic contribution of the Chinese community to the state's development. And on several occasions, he stated that Johor is home to its various ethnic communities and racist practices are forbidden.[69]

---

[66] Anthony Milner, *The Invention of Politics in Colonial Malaya: Contesting nationalism and the expansion of the public sphere* (Cambridge: Cambridge University Press, 1995) p. 198; C.S. Gray, "Johore 1910–1941: Studies in the Colonial Process" (PhD Dissertation, Yale University, 1978), pp. 142–43.

[67] A Jalil Hamid, "Concord is a Blessing", *New Straits Times*, 30 August 2016; A Jalil Hamid, "Bangsa Johor Concept now More Relevant than Ever, Says Johor Ruler", *New Straits Times*, 30 August 2016. The state's anthem, *Lagu Bangsa Johor* was composed in 1897, but its lyrics were written in 1914. They request the Sultan's protection of the state, as well as his leadership to help it attain freedom and unity <http://kemahkotaan.johor.gov.my/pengenalan/lagu-bangsa-johor/> (accessed 31 October 2016).

[68] The Chinese Hall or Dewan Cina was a gift from prominent Chinese businessmen in Johor, including Wong Ah Fook, who built the Istana Besar. Yee Xiang Yun, "Johor Ruler to Host Chinese at event last seen 65 years ago", *The Star*, 7 September 2016.

[69] "Sultan of Johor Braves Scorching Heat to Meet Devotees during Thaipusam", *The Star*, 25 January 2016; "Sultan Ibrahim the first Johor Ruler to attend Chingay procession", *The Star*, 19 January 2016; "Johor Sultan tells Racists, Haters to Get Out of his State", *Malaysian Insider*, 16 September 2015.

This wider conception of citizenship or belonging has roots in the pre-colonial era, where the subjects of a sultan were referred to collectively as "rakyat" or "people", as opposed to their specific ethnicity.[70] Furthermore, the consolidation of the rubber-based economy in the state during the early twentieth century as well as a liberal immigration policy, led to substantial inflows of people from China, India, Java, and Sumatra. After World War II, Johor had the second largest population among the territories in Malaya, behind Perak, and housed one of the country's largest Chinese populations.[71]

Records from the mid-1870s show that Sultan Abu Bakar included non-Malays in high-level decision-making bodies. Thus, he created a State Council to debate legislation and policy issues which brought together: the aristocracy, government bureaucrats, the religious establishment, and two of the most powerful Chinese businessmen. The Johor Constitution further formalized this tradition by specifying the Council's membership. Appointed by the Sultan, the members could be ministers, government officials, or community leaders of any ethnicity, but had to be Johore subjects.[72]

This tradition of consulting various ethnic groups can be seen in the discussions in 2013 between Sultan Ibrahim and the Malaysian Chinese Association (MCA) over his choice to appoint a local MCA member to the State Executive Council. The MCA leadership had declared that no party member would accept a national or state-level position, given the party's poor electoral performance in the general elections. However, Sultan Ibrahim persisted with the appointment, stating that naming members to the Executive Council was his prerogative as traditional ruler and as established in the Johor Constitution.[73]

---

[70] Milner, *The Evolution of the Malaysian Monarchy, and the Bonding of the Nation*, p. 25.

[71] M.V. Del Tufo, *A Report on the 1947 Census of Population* (London: Crown Agents for the Colonies: London, 1947).

[72] de Vere Allen, Stockwell, and Wright, *A Collection of Treaties*.

[73] "Johor Sultan Calls on All Quarters to Stop Questioning Tee's Appointment", *Sun Daily*, 1 July 2013; "Tee still an Exco Member, Stop Debating, says Sultan of Johor", *Malaysian Times*, 1 July 2013.

Johor Armed Forces

Earlier this year, the Sultan proposed that the duties of the Johor Military Force (JMF) be widened from guarding the palace grounds to monitoring administrative areas such as the state capital as well as district offices, stating that this use of existing resources would be better than hiring private firms who use foreign workers. Furthermore, he called for the state government to revive the Johor Volunteer Force (JVF) and encourage members of the Johor civil service to join it, in order to boost their spirit of volunteerism and help with disaster management and community service.[74]

Johor is the only state in Malaysia to have its own military force. In 1886, Sultan Abu Bakar established it to assert Johor's independence and reduce its reliance on British forces.[75] During the British period, the JMF remained tightly under Sultan Ibrahim's control. He used it as a means of controlling the civil service — through his ability to hire and then second JMF officers to key positions in the government — and a private police force.[76] In 1905, Sultan Ibrahim further established the Johor Volunteer Force (JVF), whose ranks drew from the civil service. In 1938, the JMF reached a peak of 1,000 troops, with a further 800 members in the JVF.[77] Mahathir did consider disbanding the JMF in the wake of the 1993 constitutional crisis, but it still exists and numbers some 200 troops.[78]

---

[74] P. Lim Pui Huen, *Johor: Local History, Local Landscapes: 1855–1957* (Singapore: Straits Times Press, 2009), p. 23; "Sultan Ibrahim Suggests Wider Scope of Duties for JMF", *Free Malaysia Today*, 8 April 2016; "Sultan Ibrahim Wants Johor Government to Revive JVF", *Malay Mail Online*, 12 May 2016.

[75] P. Lim Pui Huen, *Johor: Local History, Local Landscapes: 1855–1957*, p. 122.

[76] Gray, "Johore 1910–1941: Studies in the Colonial Process", p. 56; in 1915, Sultan Ibrahim used the JMF to quell a mutiny of Indian troops in Singapore, for which he was awarded a knighthood by the British.

[77] Gullick, *Rulers and Residents: Influence and Power in the Malay States*, p. 110; *Johore, Annual Report for 1938* (Singapore: Government Printing Office, 1939), p. 67.

[78] "KL disbands Johor Sultan's Private Army", *Straits Times*, 19 August 1993.

Public Health

Issues pertaining to religion, Malay custom, and wider issues of identity are within the current constitutional role attributed to the sultans. However, in November 2015, the Sultan ordered a ban on the sale of vaping products in Johor for health reasons. Since vaping is a public health issue, which falls under both federal and state government responsibility, questions were raised regarding the process by which the ban was declared. Experts in Malaysian constitutional law argued that the ban would need to be enacted by the State Legislative Assembly, rather than via the Sultan's decree. However, in December 2015, this issue was put to rest when the Johor State Executive Council officially banned the sale of vape products in the state.[79]

Environmental and Natural Resource Management Issues

Under the Federal Constitution, natural resources are listed as a state government responsibility, and oil and timber concessions have in fact been an important source of revenue for this level of government. In his speech before the State Legislative Assembly in May 2014, Sultan Ibrahim Ismail requested that the state government allot one fourth of its land to forest reserves, and that the awarding of logging concessions be frozen. He also suggested that a state government corporation be established to handle environmental issues, and proposed passing an enactment to allow the state government to directly approve environmental impact assessments. This contrasts with standard practice where such assessments are routed through the federal government.

The Sultan specifically cited the Benalec project, a 1,400 ha reclamation project in the Johor Strait meant to house a large oil and gas complex, which had been waiting three years for an environmental

---

[79] Federal Constitution of Malaysia, art. 74, 77, ninth schedule; Koh Jun Lin. "Johor Sultan Can't Just Decree Vape Ban, Law Experts Say", *Malaysiakini*, 29 November 2015.

impact assessment.[80] In addition, concerns were raised during this period about Forest City, an even larger land reclamation project. Led by an established Chinese developer, Country Garden, in conjunction with the Sultan and a state government-owned commercial vehicle, the project envisages creating four artificial islands collectively measuring some 2,000 hectares. Worries were raised that land reclamation had begun without an environmental impact assessment. Initial objections were raised by the Federal Department of the Environment, but both projects were eventually approved, although only partially in the case of the Forest City project.[81]

Land Management

Land management is a central part of state government work, holding great implications for zoning and real estate development. The Housing and Property Board 2014 enactment envisaged an agency to oversee the development of real property and housing in Johor. In its original form, the enactment gave the Sultan of Johor the power to appoint board members, dissolve the board and oversee its accounts.

This led to concerns from UMNO leaders, opposition members, as well as civic organizations regarding the operational role that it imagines for the Sultan. The deputy president of the opposition party PAS stated that his party "supports the constitutional role of the Malay rulers as defined by the Federal Constitution ... Efforts to give Sultan Ibrahim ... executive powers should never happen"; while UMNO party member and former Cabinet Member, Zainuddin Maidin, criticized the Menteri

---

[80] "Johor to Table State Environment Act in 2015", *Sun Daily,* 9 July 2014; Speech delivered by Sultan Ibrahim Ismail before the State Legislative Assembly of Johor, 31 May 2014.

[81] Summer Zhen, "Country Garden's Ambition in Malaysia Backed by Johor's Royal Family", *South China Morning Post,* 11 February 2016; Reme Ahmad, "Johor Reclamation Project 'To Create Oil Storage Hub'", *Straits Times,* 27 June 2014; "No EIA, but Johor Coastal Reclamation Projects already Underway, Say Sources", *Malaysian Insider,* 23 June 2014; Shannon Teoh, "Malaysia gives Nod for Johor Reclamation Project but Cuts Size", *Straits Times,* 6 January 2015.

Besar, stating that he "should have acknowledged that the power of the people is greater than the power of the monarchy and not proceeded with the tabling". The Malaysian Bar Council cautioned the state government that granting such far-reaching administrative powers to the ruler would expose him to criticism.[82]

The state government eventually decided to amend the enactment to limit the Sultan's power to the right to appoint only four board members, subject to the advice of the Menteri Besar. The language of the provisions was also changed such that the powers would be vested in the "state authorities" rather than in the Johor "Ruler". The Sultan initially gave his assurance that he would not interfere in state executive matters but he maintained that he could only endorse the bill once state authorities had travelled around the state to explain the provisions of the enactment to Johoreans.[83]

A year later, the Sultan called for a review of the enactment, stating that it "… was amended through pressure from outsiders who were narrow minded … and do not understand the power of the ruler in Johor's state constitution". While the bill was passed by the state legislative assembly in June 2014, the Sultan has not yet officially endorsed the enactment.[84]

National-level Issues

Beyond the policy issues highlighted above, Sultan Ibrahim Ismail has also spoken out on a number of national-level issues. While these do not entail an operational role, they do raise important questions, not least about the role played by the monarchy itself.

---

[82] Yong Yen Nie, "Johor Housing Bill Amended after Uproar over Sultan's Powers", *Straits Times*, 9 June 2014; "Bar Wants Johor Bill Amended to Avoid Opening Sultan to Attack", *Malaysia Today*, 8 June 2014; S. Jayasankaran, "Controversial Johor bill passed after key changes", *Business Times*, 10 June 2014.

[83] Yong Yen Nie, "Johor Sultan 'Will not Interfere' in Matters of State Govt", *Straits Times*, 13 June 2014.

[84] Othman, Ahmad Fairuz, "Johor Sultan calls for the Johor Real Property and Housing Board Bill review", *New Straits Times*, 7 May 2015.

English Standards

The Sultan has, on several occasions, called for the Malaysian government to improve the standard of English in the education system and suggested that Singapore be examined as a model. In addition, he has stated that the country's various language streams have resulted in non-Malays not being able to speak Malay, and in Malays being unable to speak English.[85] Beyond the issues of educational quality that this raises, rectifying this would also mean completely reconfiguring the education system at the primary level, and switching the medium of instruction at the secondary level.

Again, this statement is based on Johor's unique history and long-standing emphasis on both English and Malay education. English medium schools were established in Johor as early as in 1864, and the first Malay school was established in 1878. The education department was established five years later, and in 1884, Sultan Abu Bakar decreed that every district in the state should have a school. In 1902, Sultan Ibrahim issued a proclamation which required all households of Johore, regardless of race, to send their male children between seven and sixteen years of age to school.[86]

Indeed, the education system constituted one of the areas of greatest conflict between the Sultan and the British, with the former in favour of widespread education in English and the latter supporting generalized Malay-medium schools with limited provision of English education for a reduced number. The Sultan finally relinquished direct control over the education system, with the exception of religious education, in 1928.[87] Due to its high levels of government revenue and commitment

---

[85] "Johor Sultan slams Malaysia's Multi-stream Schools", *Straits Times*, 29 October 2015; "Make English a Medium of Instruction in Schools: Sultan of Johor", *AsiaOne*, 12 June 2015; Wong Chun Wai and Nelson Benjamin, "English, the Universal Currency", *Star Online*, 12 June 2015.

[86] P. Lim Pui Huen, *Johor: Local History, Local Landscapes: 1855–1957*, p. 146.

[87] Khoo Kay Kim, "Sultan Ibrahim's Reign (up to 1941)", in R.O. Winstedt, *A History of Johore (1365–1941)* (Selangor: MBRAS, 2003), p. 159.

to education, Johor had one of the highest levels of literacy among the Malay States in the 1940s.[88]

Relations with Singapore

In recent years, Sultan Ibrahim Ismail has advocated for the Johor state government to play a more active role in Malaysia's relationship with Singapore. His statements have revolved around a number of issues, including: replacing the Causeway to alleviate heavy traffic flowing to and from Singapore as well as increasing mobility; the status of Pedra Branca, over which conflicting claims by Singapore and Malaysia were largely resolved by the International Court of Justice; and connecting Johor Bahru and Singapore via public transport.[89]

The Sultan has argued that while bilateral relations are a federal responsibility, national leaders should at least consider Johor's views when they craft policies towards Singapore, due to the state's deep understanding of its neighbour, as well as its own sentiment and legal precedent on particular issues. In line with these, he has also offered to mediate on bilateral issues.[90]

While not fitting into the current federal allocation of responsibilities, bilateral relations between Johor and Singapore have deep historical roots. Indeed, it was the Sultanate that contributed the greatest part of the funds to build the Causeway linking Johor with Singapore in 1923. Initially intended solely to connect Singapore to the Federated Malay States by rail, Sultan Ibrahim agreed to contribute additional funds for

---

[88] Del Tufo, *A Report on the 1947 Census of Population*, Table 52.

[89] "Johor Sultan: Consider Replacing the Causeway", *AsiaOne,* 23 March 2016; "Johor Diminta Tubuh Pasukan Rayuan Keputusan Pulau Batu Putih" [Johor requests to form a team to appeal the decision regarding Pulau Batu Putih], *Utusan Online*, 30 May 2014; Speech delivered by Sultan Ibrahim Ismail before the State Legislative Assembly of Johor, 31 May 2014; "Learn from S'pore Education Policy, Johor Sultan Says", *Straits Times*, 13 June 2015.

[90] "Johor Sultan Willing to Mediate on Bilateral Issues", *Straits Times*, 8 March 2010; "It Will Be Insane to Tell Investor Not to Come to Johor", *New Straits Times,* 22 March 2015.

it to be open to pedestrians and other vehicles. All in all, the Sultanate contributed more than $3.2 million of the total $4.8 million that the project cost.[91]

The Sultanate also made substantial contributions to Singapore's defence in the colonial era. In February 1915, when the Indian 5th Light Infantry guarding German internees at Tanglin Barracks mutinied, Sultan Ibrahim himself led JMF reinforcements to Singapore to help quell the mutiny.[92] In 1935, amid an atmosphere of growing Japanese aggression in the region, Sultan Ibrahim gifted the colonial government in Singapore with £500,000 to celebrate King George V's Silver Jubilee, specifying that the money should be used to accelerate work on the Singapore naval base.[93] £400,000 of the gift was used to install two of the three 15-inch guns of the Johore battery in Changi. These were the biggest guns outside Britain during World War II.[94]

Furthermore, Sultan Ibrahim signed the first water agreement between Johor and Singapore in 1927, which then formed the basis for the 1961 and 1962 water agreements between Singapore and Malaysia. The demarcation of the border between Singapore and Johor was made through negotiations between the British Crown and the Sultan in 1928. The agreement resolved the contradiction concerning the ten-mile limit around Singapore by giving the Sultan of Johor control over islets and waters within three miles of Johor. If this had not been done, all the Johor Strait and certain areas in the southwest and southeast would have remained under the control of Singapore even though they were closer to Johor.[95]

---

[91] State of Johore, *A Souvenir Commemorating the Diamond Jubilee of His Highness the Sultan of Johore*, 1955, p. 20.

[92] P. Lim Pui Huen, *Johor: Local History, Local Landscapes: 1855–1957*, p. 127.

[93] "Prime Minister and Johore's Jubilee Gift", *Straits Times*, 5 June 1935.

[94] Jenny Kiong and Chan Fook Weng, "Johore Battery", National Library Board, 2010, <http://eresources.nlb.gov.sg/infopedia/articles/SIP_1073_2010-05-07.html> (accessed 1 November 2016).

[95] Straits Settlements and Johore Territorial Waters (Agreement) Act, 1928, Colony of the Straits Settlements and Sultan of the State and Territory of Johore, 19 October 1927. Lee Yong Leng, *The Razor's Edge: Boundaries and Boundary Dispute in Southeast Asia* (Singapore: Institute of Southeast Asian Studies, 1980).

The Role of the Monarchy

Earlier this year, Sultan Ibrahim Ismail stated that Malaysia should repeal the constitutional amendments of 1993 which curtailed the prerogatives of traditional rulers and removed their legal immunity. In his opinion, these have reduced the role of the sultans to that of mere rubber stampers for laws passed by Parliament or the various state legislative assemblies. He stated that "It is not proper to limit or abolish the power of the King or the Sultan in examining and giving their Royal Assent for laws", and the constitutional amendments "grabbed the powers of the King for the sake of political or individual interest".[96]

In light of the wide range of policy matters that the Sultan has sought to influence, these remarks further indicate that he advocates a more traditional role and a wider ranging mandate for the Rulers. One constitutional expert has stated that there is legal basis for this challenge before the Federal Court, as the 1993 constitutional amendments did not have the assent of the Conference of Rulers.[97]

CONCLUSIONS

The Sultan of Johor has assumed a very visible local and national political role, based on a very specific understanding of what the role of a traditional ruler should be. In its ceremonial aspects, it is rooted in the pre-colonial era, when sultans played a very public role deeply entrenched in symbolism. In its policy-related aspects, it is inspired by the state-building achievements of two previous sultans, who developed key aspects of Johor's state apparatus and preserved its autonomy.

This more expansive role stands in contrast to the tenor of political life since the early 1980s which has seen the rulers adopt a lower public profile. However, over the last decade, the sultans have been attempting to exercise their prerogatives more frequently. This seems to be part of

---

[96] Shannon Teoh, "Johor Sultan Calls for Restoration of Monarchs' Powers", *Straits Times*, 9 May 2016.

[97] "Johor Sultan can Challenge 1994 Constitutional Restrictions on this Power, says Law Expert", *Malaysian Insider*, 7 May, 2015.

a continuing process where the precise contours of the sultans' roles fluctuate.

The Sultan's various policy positions and initiatives have not gone uncontested, and there has been push-back. Political heavyweights such as Musa Hitam and Mahathir Mohamed were vocal in their opposition to the operational role framed for the Sultan in the proposed Housing and Property Board. Mahathir also disagreed with the concept of Bangsa Johor, stating that it could lead to feelings of superiority among certain sectors of society and could potentially lead to the breakup of the Malaysian Federation. This was subsequently rebutted by the Sultan.[98]

Minister for Tourism and Culture Nazri Aziz pointedly advised the Crown Prince to refrain from politics following the latter's criticism of Prime Minister Najib Razak. He stated that, should the Prince get involved in politics, he would get "whacked". He then referred to the classic contest for leadership between princes and politicians, and how politicians "are the ones protecting the royalty". The Crown Prince rejected this, subsequently raising the possibility of Johor seceding, and then posting a statement on Facebook calling upon critics of Johor to ask Prime Minister Najib to expel the state from the federation.[99]

Initiatives proposed by the Sultan of Johor for the future include establishing a Bank of Johor to provide credit to the state's residents; building a maglev train linking the eastern and western parts of Johor Bahru; and implementing a public housing scheme.[100] He also called for the federal government to address the economic situation facing the

[98] A. Jalil Hamid, "Concord is a Blessing", *New Straits Times*, 30 August 2016.

[99] "Johor Prince posts Defiant Video after Minister's Warning", *Sunday Times*, 14 June 2015; "Johor Crown Prince Warns that State May Secede if Putrajaya Breaches Federation's Terms", *Straits Times*, 16 October 2015; "Critics should ask Najib to Expel Johor from Malaysia, Says Crown Prince", *AsiaOne*, 2 June 2016.

[100] A. Jalil Hamid, "Concord is a Blessing", *New Straits Times*, 30 August 2016; A. Jalil Hamid, "Bangsa Johor Concept now more Relevant than Ever, Says Johor Ruler", *New Straits Times*, 30 August 2016.

country, including the falling value of the ringgit.[101] Regarding the current position of the Rulers, he has lamented the passage of the constitutional amendments, advocating their repeal and stating that "Johor has a mission. The mission is to restore the 'order'."[102]

---

[101] "Don't Make a Fool of Raykat", *New Paper*, 26 August 2015.

[102] "Malay Leaders Used to Defend Powers of Monarchy, Not Any More", *Malaysiakini*, 7 May 2016.